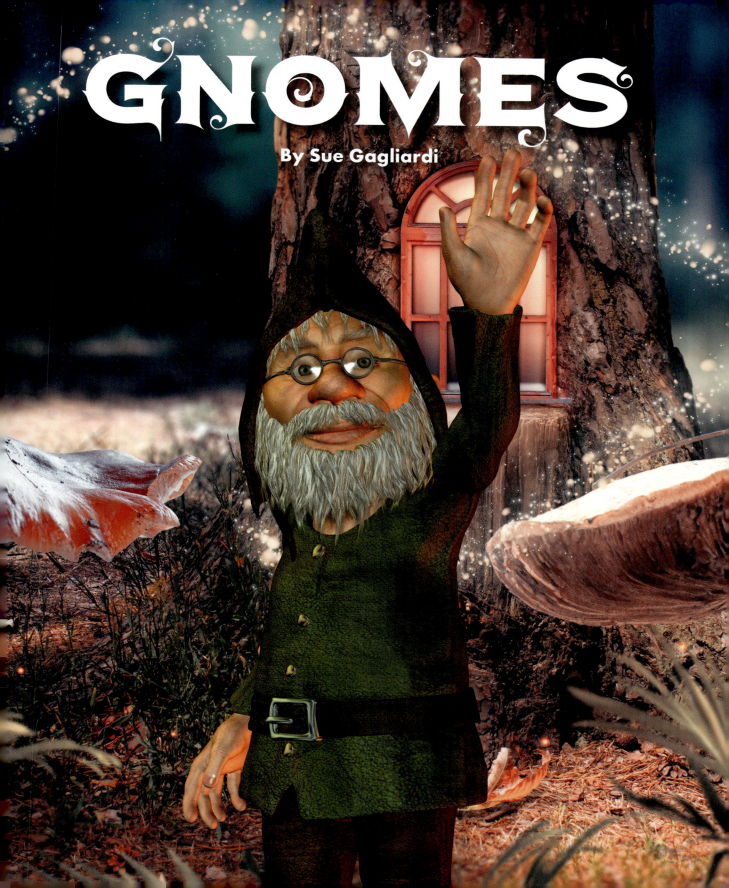

Published by The Child's World®
1980 Lookout Drive • Mankato, MN 56003-1705
800-599-READ • www.childsworld.com

Photographs ©: Shutterstock Images, cover (gnome), 1 (gnome), 7, 9, 11, 13 (gnome), 23; Julia Ardaran/Shutterstock Images, cover (background), 1–3 (background); iStockphoto, 5, 24; Fang Xia Nuo/iStockphoto, 6; Natalia Bratslavsky/Shutterstock Images, 10; Valdis Skudre/Shutterstock Images, 13 (background); Ralf Juergen Kraft/Shutterstock Images, 14; Gwen Vidig/iStockphoto, 15; Sarunyu L./Shutterstock Images, 17; Salwan Georges/The Washington Post/Getty Images, 18; Philippe Clement/Shutterstock Images, 20–21

Copyright © 2022 by The Child's World®
All rights reserved. No part of this book may be reproduced or utilized in any form or by any means without written permission from the publisher.

ISBN 9781503850309 (Reinforced Library Binding)
ISBN 9781503850798 (Portable Document Format)
ISBN 9781503851559 (Online Multi-user eBook)
LCCN 2021939352

Printed in the United States of America

Table of CONTENTS

CHAPTER ONE
Gnomes in the Garden...4

CHAPTER TWO
History of Gnomes...8

CHAPTER THREE
How Gnomes Look and Act...12

CHAPTER FOUR
Gnomes Today...16

Glossary...22

To Learn More...23

Index...24

CHAPTER ONE
GNOMES IN THE GARDEN

Lily and her grandmother stepped into the garden. It was filled with flowers and vegetables. Lily explored along the garden path.

She discovered treasures hidden among the flowers. She saw statues of frogs and turtles. There were some unusual statues tucked in the flower beds, too. They looked like little people with beards and pointed hats. They wore bright clothes. They carried lanterns and little shovels.

Some people fill their gardens with statues and decorations.

Stories and legends can be passed down through families.

Lily asked her grandmother about the statues. Her grandmother told her they were called garden gnomes. Lily wanted to know more about them. Her grandmother dug out a book. They sat on a bench beneath the tree and read.

Lily read that legends about gnomes have existed for hundreds of years. Stories tell of mythical creatures that take care of the earth. She learned that these creatures live underground and help people. In some European countries, some people believe gnomes **tend** gardens at night. People keep gnome statues in their gardens. The statues remind people of the legends about gnomes. Lily knew that gnomes were not real. But she was happy to imagine them tending her grandmother's garden.

Legends say gnomes take care of gardens, so garden gnomes became popular.

CHAPTER TWO

HISTORY OF GNOMES

People have told stories about gnomes for hundreds of years. In the 1500s, a Swiss doctor and writer named Paracelsus wrote stories about small creatures who lived underground. He called these creatures gnomes. The name *gnome* means "earth **dweller**."

Stories about gnomes are told in many parts of the world. In British **folklore**, gnomes travel in the evenings. They have eyes like cats or owls. They can see well at night as they work in the garden. They are skilled at hiding.

In some stories, gnomes live inside mushrooms.

In Polish stories, gnomes live in mines. The Wieliczka Salt Mine in Poland has statues of gnomes along its tourist route.

In Russian and Polish stories, gnomes live in **clans**. They live in the mountains and in underground mines. Some stories say if daylight shines on gnomes, they can get confused or turn to stone. Many gnomes **inhabit** hollow trees.

Gnome stories are also common in **Scandinavia**. In Norway, gnomes are called *nisse* (NEE-seh). They wear red pointed caps. Nisse live in trees and inside human homes and barns. According to legends, nisse do chores for humans during the night. They clean and work in the fields. Nisse are neat and tidy. Humans reward them with gifts of porridge and butter. Nisse love to dance and play music. They teach humans how to play the fiddle. They bring good luck. But if humans upset them, nisse will leave and take the good luck with them.

Scandinavian gnomes are common decorations.

CHAPTER THREE
HOW GNOMES LOOK AND ACT

According to German folklore, gnomes look like small humans. Their size ranges from 1 to 3.3 feet (.3 to 1 m) tall. Male gnomes have thick hair and beards. Their hands and feet are often covered with dirt. They are strong and muscular. They wear hats and leather coats. Female gnomes are smaller than male gnomes.

In some regions, gnomes have physical features that fit their personalities. In German stories, nosy gnomes have six pairs of eyes. Greedy gnomes have four mouths. Quick gnomes have eight feet.

In Russian legends, gnomes are clumsy and stumble often. Their bodies are smeared with black dirt. Their hands and feet look like tree roots. They have long eyelids that almost reach the ground.

hat

beard

1 to 3.3 feet (.3 to 1 m) tall

Stories often say gnomes look similar to humans.

leather clothes

In some legends, gnomes can shrink to fit through narrow openings. In other stories, gnomes can disappear into the earth. They can move through soil as if it were air.

Some people believe gnomes use their secret magic to help humans. For example, they help people find underground **resources** such as metal and precious stones. Gnomes also work as miners, bakers, and gardeners in the human world. They bake cakes flavored with cave plants. They grow mushrooms to eat. They raise goats for milk and meat. They polish metal and stones. They work in the garden at night.

In stories, gnomes have an important connection to nature.

According to the legends, gnomes know the secrets of the earth. They can bring animals and plants to life. They can communicate with flowers, animals, and fairy creatures. They guard the earth's treasures.

CHAPTER FOUR

GNOMES TODAY

Gnomes are part of popular culture today. Gnome stories are featured in books and movies. They also appear in special celebrations in different parts of the world.

Gnome characters are seen in popular movies. The movie *Gnomeo and Juliet* features garden gnomes who come to life. *Sherlock Gnomes* is another movie with garden gnome characters. The gnomes in this movie are detectives.

In Sherlock Gnomes, Gnomeo and Juliet hire Sherlock to solve a mystery.

Dawson is a small town known for creating gnome statues of its residents.

Some places have special gnome celebrations. In Dawson, Minnesota, people tell gnome stories from Germany and Scandinavia. Dawson is nicknamed Gnometown. The town honors a resident each year. The resident receives a gnome statue. People who help their community are selected for the honor. The statues are on display in the town's Gnome Park. Dawson's website features stories about all of the gnomes.

In England, people can visit the Gnome Reserve. Visitors can see more than 2,000 garden gnomes along the garden paths. The garden has one of the largest garden gnome collections in the world.

Garden gnomes continue to delight gardeners.

People continue to tell stories about gnomes. People pass these stories down through generations. These legendary creatures are part of the history and culture of many countries.

GLOSSARY

clans (KLANZ) Clans are groups of people who live and work together. Gnomes in some stories live in clans.

dweller (DWEL-lur) A dweller is a person or animal who lives in a certain place. The word *gnome* means "earth dweller," and stories about gnomes say they live underground.

folklore (FOHK-lohr) Folklore is the stories and beliefs that a group of people have passed down through the generations. Gnomes appear in folklore from several different countries.

inhabit (in-HAB-uht) To inhabit means to live in a place. Gnomes inhabit mines and hollow trees.

resources (REE-sor-sez) Resources are a source of supplies or needed items. Gnomes helped humans find resources such as metal and precious stones.

Scandinavia (scan-dih-NAY-vee-uh) Scandinavia refers to the countries of Norway, Sweden, and Denmark, and sometimes Finland and Iceland. Gnome stories are common in Scandinavia.

tend (TEND) To tend something means to take care of it and help it grow. Some people believe that garden gnomes tend gardens at night.

TO LEARN MORE

In the Library

Bell, Samantha S. *Build a Compact Garden*. Mankato, MN: The Child's World, 2017.

Mara, Wil. *Norway*. New York, NY: Children's Press, 2017.

Owen, Ruth. *I Can Grow a Garden!* New York, NY: Windmill Books, 2018.

On the Web

Visit our website for links about gnomes:

childsworld.com/links

Note to Parents, Teachers, and Librarians: We routinely verify our Web links to make sure they are safe and active sites. So encourage your readers to check them out!

INDEX

appearance, 4, 11, 12

Dawson, Minnesota, 19

gardens, 4–7, 8, 14, 20
Germany, 12, 19
Gnomeo and Juliet, 16

mushrooms, 14

nisse, 11

powers, 7, 8, 11, 14–15

Russia, 10, 12

Scandinavia, 11, 19
statues, 4–7, 16, 19–20

ABOUT THE AUTHOR

Sue Gagliardi writes fiction, nonfiction, and poetry for children. Her work appears in many different magazines for children. She teaches third grade and lives in Pennsylvania with her husband and son.